Books by Munro Leaf

THE WISHING POOL
SCIENCE CAN BE FUN
MANNERS CAN BE FUN
THREE PROMISES TO YOU
LUCKY YOU
READING CAN BE FUN
GEOGRAPHY CAN BE FUN
HISTORY CAN BE FUN
ARITHMETIC CAN BE FUN
HOW TO BEHAVE AND WHY
FLOCK OF WATCHBIRDS
LET'S DO BETTER
GORDON THE GOAT
HEALTH CAN BE FUN
JOHN HENRY DAVIS
FAIR PLAY
SAFETY CAN BE FUN
ROBERT FRANCIS WEATHERBEE
GRAMMAR CAN BE FUN

HEALTH CAN BE FUN

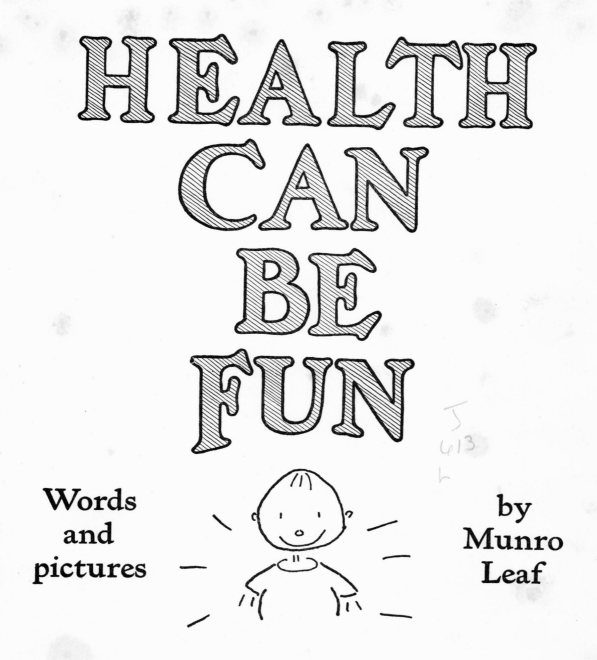

Words
and
pictures

by
Munro
Leaf

J. B. LIPPINCOTT COMPANY

PHILADELPHIA   NEW YORK

Fourteenth Printing

20035

Library of Congress catalog card number 43-13211

PRINTED IN THE UNITED STATES OF AMERICA

GOOD HEALTH

is something we don't think

about very much

until

WE

DON'T

HAVE

IT.

Then, when we
are sick and
feel awful, we
promise ourselves
that we will take
better care of our

HEALTH

as soon as we get well.

BUT

when we do feel better
again, too many of us
just forget all about
it.

That is a foolish way to

behave and as

long as we act

like that we shall probably

keep right on being

sick or weak or wobbly

a lot of the time.

BECAUSE

STAYING
HEALTHY

is a game we

have to play all

the time,

not just once in a

while.

When we are

BABIES

Somebody has to see that

we have the right

food and clothes

and that we get
exercise and fresh air

that we are kept clean

and have enough
rest and sleep.

SOMEBODY ELSE HAS TO TAKE
CARE OF ALL THAT FOR US
But—
As we grow older and bigger we learn
more and more
until after a while
we know how
to take care of ourselves.

We know why we must

drink some things and

eat some things

to make our bodies

grow

stronger and better.

First
We find out about the

we drink.

It comes from cows

and it is the best food or
drink for us that
anybody has ever found
anywhere in the world.
Milk has in it more different things
than any other single food or drink
that will
build strong muscles
and
good bones and teeth
and
give us energy and pep
all at the same time.

It has sugar and fats that we need and
vitamins that help to keep us well.
Milk is a food that costs so little and

gives us so much that we can see why
the best doctors tell us that we should
drink a quart of it every day.
When we KNOW things like that
we don't have to have people
nag at us and scold and beg to get us
to drink milk.

But we know too that as good as

milk is for us, it still isn't enough.

We couldn't get along as growing

boys and girls on just milk alone.

We need to eat bread and meat, fish

and eggs,

fresh vegetables, fruits,

cereals and other foods to

build strong, healthy bodies.

And if there is one creature
that makes everybody tired
it's a

FOOD GRUMBLER

that

won't eat what

is good for it—

and mumbles and grumbles
about eating anything except
just what it thinks it
likes.
It won't eat this and it won't eat that
until people get so tired of it they almost
don't care what happens to it at all.

Even when we eat the same
food, all of us don't grow to be
the same size and
shape.

Some of us are
tall, some short,
some heavier
than others and some lighter. But all

of us don't want to do the
same things and be exactly
alike, so it is a
good thing
that we are
different.

We do want to be well and

healthy though, so that no matter what

size we are or what we do,

we can be

helpful to others and happy

ourselves.

EXERCISE

One of the best ways to keep ourselves

healthy is to get plenty of good

exercise.

To move around out in the fresh air

every day, working

and playing,

is the best way to stretch muscles
and make them grow.
Boys and girls who just sit around
all the time are never as healthy
as others and they don't
have as much fun
either.

If you just flop and mope around
like a lump, and never run or
jump or ride or walk fast with
your head up and your shoulders
back, you will miss a lot.
And don't be surprised if you grow up

to be a dull soggy
person who is about
as much fun to
be with as a bag
of wet sand.

Whatever kind of exercise you take at work or play try to remember that you will be a lot

more comfortable, healthy, and better looking if you aren't a

STOOPER

that walks around with its shoulders so bent over it looks like a monkey-----

or a SLOUCHER

that sits down as though its seat were

up in the middle of its back.

REST AND SLEEP

One of the most important things
we have to do to stay healthy
is to get enough
REST

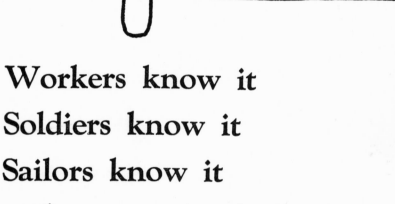

Workers know it
Soldiers know it
Sailors know it
and even animals know it.

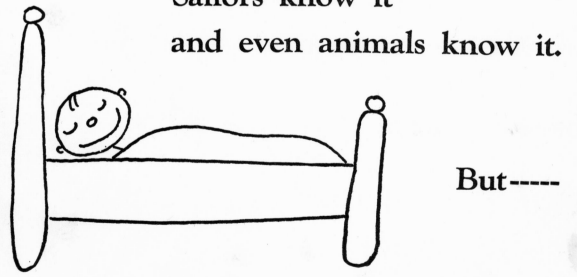

But-----

Some Boys   and Girls

who should know that we

need to rest the most while we are

still growing

Scream and yell

or

 Moan and groan

or

pout and whine

like tiny babies when it is

time to take a

nap or go to bed

at night.

That makes more people

angry than almost

anything else that stupid

children do.

It is as bad manners to

cry and argue about going

to bed when we should

as it is unhealthy.

So

GO TO BED

when you should

and STOP fussing about it

like a two year old.

When you sleep

be sure that you have some

fresh air in your room.

That doesn't mean you have to freeze

the place and have drafts blowing

through it, but it wants to be well aired

and ventilated for the best sleeping.

KEEPING
CLEAN

if we

kept ourselves

clean

just to look better it would

be worth doing

But

there are more important reasons

than that for

keeping ourselves clean.

DIRT   and   GERMS that

make us

sick

go together

and

WORK TOGETHER

27

IF WE
WANT TO STAY HEALTHY
AND WELL

WE HAVE TO WASH
OURSELVES
REGULARLY

NOT JUST

SOAP

WASH CLOTH

OUR FACES

BUT

Our Hands
most of all

and

all the rest

of our

bodies

sometimes.

DO YOU KNOW WHY?

Because

in all dirt there are GERMS.

They are tiny live things, so

little we can't even see them,

 unless we look at them

through a microscope,

but they are there just the same.

Some Germs are Disease Germs
that make us sick if they get
inside us.

They get into us mostly through
our mouths and noses,
but they can go in through
our skin too.

SO

if we keep ourselves clean
and get the dirt off us
the germs have less
chance to get inside.

When we eat we often touch the food that goes inside us and if our hands are full of dirt and germs, even if we can't see them, there they go right into our mouths.

That is why we always try to wash our hands before we eat.

And just count how many times you put your hands up to your mouth and nose and you will see why it makes good sense to keep them clean.

BATHS

Make us clean all over

on the outside

And we must

not forget

that

It is just as important for

us to be clean

INSIDE

If we are to stay healthy

and well.

The FOOD we eat
gets all divided up inside
us.
Some of it goes to make
muscle and to build our
bodies bigger and stronger.
Some goes to make teeth and
strengthen our bones, some
for hair and fingernails and
toenails and all parts of us.
The part of the food that
isn't any good for us and
is just waste goes on
through our bodies and
we get rid of it.

That is why we go to the
toilet.
If this old waste food stayed
inside us too long it would
make us sick too.
So it is very important that
at least once every day we
go to the toilet to get rid
of this old waste food.
And remember this.
After we have gone to the toilet
We should be very
sure to WASH
OUR HANDS

TEETH

We get two sets of teeth,

and we need to take good care of them

First we get our

Baby teeth.

One or two at a time.

These usually start to come when

we are about 6 or 8 months old.

We get our 4 big back

teeth

and as our grown up teeth come

in our front baby teeth come

out.

It is very important for us
to keep our teeth clean
so they will be healthy
and not decay.

If we take good care of our first
baby teeth, then our grown up
teeth will come in straighter and
stronger.

Then we have to be sure to
keep our grown up teeth
well cleaned because
they are the last
ones we will ever
get.

Nobody ever gets more than 2 sets
of real teeth. So
Take Care of them.

Be Sure

To brush them

in the morning and every night

before you go to bed.

Many people think it is

very wise to brush

them after every meal.

If you have a dentist look at

your teeth twice every year, you

won't have so many toothaches

and you will keep your

teeth longer.

HAIR AND FINGERNAILS

Our hair and our fingernails
need to be kept clean
and cut

unless YOU
WANT TO BE A MESSY
AND
LOOK LIKE ONE.

And don't forget your
Toenails, just
because they happen
to be hidden by your
socks and shoes in the daytime.

CLOTHES

The clothes we wear have
a lot to do with our
health.

Clean clothes are healthy clothes.
It won't do us very much good to
take a bath if we put dirty
clothes back on us.

Some people are just too lazy
to change their clothes as
often as they should
and somebody has to nag

at them all the time to
make them do it.
That gets tiresome and anybody
with any real sense would change his
or her clothes without all that squawking
--- and everybody would feel better.

When it is cold we wear more clothes to keep us warm.

That is simple and almost anybody can understand why we do that.

BUT

the thing just as simple that a lot of people don't seem to understand is that it is just as dangerous to be too warm as it is to be too cold.

When we come into heated houses in the winter we should take off the heavy clothes that we wear outdoors.

If we don't we get too warm and the next time we go out, we are very likely to catch a cold.

More people are sick from catching COLDS than from any other

disease. We catch them by breathing in the Germs that are spread by other people who have colds, or from getting chilled after being too warm, or sitting

or sleeping in a draft or getting our shoes or clothes wet and cold and not changing them soon enough.

If we take care to stay away
from people who sneeze and cough
and if we dress sensibly
and wear rubbers or overshoes
when there is rain or snow
we are not so likely to
catch colds.
When we do catch a cold
then is the time we should
take extra good care of
ourselves.

First

We want to get well ourselves

because it is no

fun to have a cold

and

Second

We don't want to give them

to other people.

To get well ourselves there

are so many things we can

do to make us feel better,

but the most important

is to STAY IN BED AND

REST FOR AT LEAST ONE

WHOLE DAY AND NIGHT.

Just having a cold by itself
isn't so very dangerous
and if we take good
care of ourselves we can usually
be well in about 7 or 9 days.
BUT the
reason we have to be so careful
is that when we have a cold
we are very likely to
catch some other kind
of disease.
Colds make us weaker than we usually
are and if we don't do what we
should we may catch
something else and be
sick for a
long time.

So
if you feel hot and stuffy and
your nose is runny, and you
start to sneeze or cough

Don't keep it a secret.
Tell the people who
take care of you and
do the right things
to get rid of it as
soon as you can.

While you are sneezing or coughing
be sure to cover your

nose and mouth so that

you won't spread your

Cold Germs for other people to breathe.
Nobody is going to thank you for giving
him or her a cold.

CUTS   SCRATCHES
BURNS   BLISTERS

and
POISON IVY.

There are lots of little things
that happen to
us all the time
like getting

scratched or cut or raising a blister,
catching poison ivy or being
stung by mosquitoes that raise
bumps on us.   For every one of these
there is a right and a wrong thing to
do and your job is to
let grown-ups know what
has happened to you so they

can be sure you get the

right care.

We don't know enough about

medicine to be sure which

ones we should use

for what.

But

Those of us who are smart

know that we should tell

others when something

is wrong with us.

Sometimes we need to
see a doctor.

Doctors are people who
have studied and worked
a long time to learn
how to make us
well again when we are
sick.
They know better than we do
what we should do.
So if
we are wise we learn to
know our Doctors as
our friends and do
what they tell us to when
they are helping us.

Some stupid people think that
staying healthy is a
sad and gloomy thing.
They sit around and
mope and worry about
how they feel all the
time.
When they feel all right
they worry because they
are afraid they won't
be well the next day.
That is just plain
Silly and Stupid.

STAYING HEALTHY

is
a
game
we
play

all the time.
Being smart
and
using

our
brains

to do
the

simple, right things
every day
will keep us

STRONG and HAPPY

because

HEALTH CAN BE FUN.